SCIENCE IN OUR WORLD

FALLING

Contributory Author
Brian Knapp, BSc, PhD
Art Director
Duncan McCrae
Special photography
Graham Servante
Special models
Tim Fulford, Head of CDT, Leighton Park School
Editorial consultants
Anna Grayson, Rita Owen
Science advisor
Jack Brettle, BSc, PhD, Chief Research Scientist,
Pilkington plc
Environmental Education Advisor
Colin Harris, County Advisor, Herts. CC
Illustrators
David Hardy and Mark Franklin
Production controller
Gillian Gatehouse
Print consultants
Landmark Production Consultants Ltd
Printed and bound in Hong Kong

Designed and produced by EARTHSCAPE EDITIONS,

First published in the United Kingdom in 1991
by Atlantic Europe Publishing Company Ltd,
86 Peppard Road, Sonning Common, Reading,
Berkshire, RG4 9RP, UK

Copyright © 1991
Atlantic Europe Publishing Company Ltd

British Library Cataloguing in Publication Data

Knapp, Brian
  Falling
  1. Gravity – For children
  I. Title   II. Series
  531
        ISBN 1-869860-40-3

Acknowledgements
The publishers would like to thank the following:
Redlands County Primary School
and Leighton Park School

Picture credits
t=top b= bottom l=left r=right

All photographs from the Earthscape Editions
photographic library except the following:
Allsport 6b; NASA 4t, 4l, 5b, 9t, 39b, 44t,
45t, 45b; NHPA 30; ZEFA 8, 9b, 21t,
22, 27t, 28b, 33t, 37, 38/39, 43

In this book you will find some
words that have been shown in
bold type. There is a full
explanation of each of these
words on pages 46 and 47.

On many pages you will find
experiments that you might
like to try for yourself. They
have been put in a coloured
box like this.

Contents

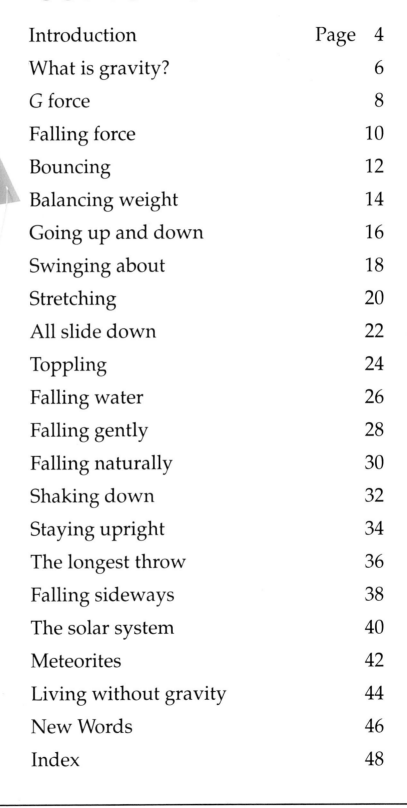

Introduction

swings
page 18

satellites
page 38

water
page 26

springs
page 20

Let a pencil drop to the ground. Throw a ball and watch its curved journey to the ground. Everywhere around us is an unseen **force** pulling things to the ground. We know it is there and it affects everything we do. It is called **gravity**.

The gravity that we feel always pulls things towards the centre of the Earth. This is why, if you let something go, it falls to the ground.

When in **space** there is little gravity inside a space ship and objects just float about out of control unless they are fastened down.

G force
page 8

winged seeds
page 30

meteorites
page 42

Solar System
page 40

throwing
page 36

balancing
page 14

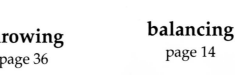

shaking down

falling force

lifts

gentle fall

dominoes

It is easier to work with gravity than against it. For example putting down a heavy parcel is easier than lifting it.

We cannot remove the force of gravity but we can make it work for us. To do this we make sure we can control the way things fall. We can make falling water give us electricity and a falling axe cut a tree down; we can have fun on a slide and even tell the time.

In this book you can discover the fascinating world of gravity in any way you choose. Just turn to a page and begin your discoveries.

centre of gravity

weightless

bouncing

falling

sliding

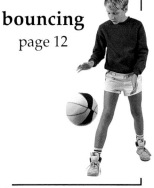

What is falling?

Falling is an experience we feel when we drop suddenly without anything to support us. Diving or jumping is a fall you have decided to make.

Newton's discovery
Sir Isaac Newton, a scientist who lived three hundred years ago, explained the falling force which we call gravity.

Newton said that because things fall there must be some unseen force – gravity – pulling them down.

It is gravity that stops us from falling off the earth and gives the planets their positions in the **Universe**.

Paragliders
Paragliding is a sport where people jump from an aeroplane and then fall hundreds of metres before they open their parachutes. As these people fall they spread their arms to slow their fall, or bring them close to their bodies to speed up.

Falling test

You might like to ask your friends whether they could make a marble and a feather reach the ground at the same time.

A falling marble only reaches the ground more quickly because it is not held back by the air. It is not because it is heavier. The feather is like the outstretched arms of a paraglider whereas the marble is like a diver who falls head first.

If you could screw up the feather into a small ball it would reach the ground at the same time as the marble. In an airless jar the marble and the feather fall at the same rate.

Same apples, different weights

Newton said that the larger the object, the more its gravity would be. The Earth is much bigger than the Moon and its gravity is therefore much greater.

If you took a kilo of apples up to the Moon and reweighed them the balance would only read 200 grammes! The amount (called the **mass**) of apples, weighs differently because there is a different value for gravity.

G force

The force of gravity on our bodies is often called the G force. The normal force that keeps us on the ground has a size of 1. But there are times when we can feel much stronger forces.

Extra G

There are many times when you can feel an extra force on your body. For example, you are pushed back in your seat whenever a car pulls away, or accelerates, quickly. These forces are not usually very great.

You can experience quite large gravitational forces on some fairground rides.

The roller coaster

The roller coaster consists of a track and small passenger cars. The cars are hauled to one side of a slope and then allowed to fall down the other side of the slope.

As the passengers hurtle down the track they feel a force which is at least twice the normal force of gravity. The extra force makes their bodies feel very heavy, pulls all their skin out of shape gives them long faces.

The extra force only lasts for a few seconds. Human bodies cannot stand up to this extra force for long.

Into space

The greatest G force is felt by astronauts as they lift off from the ground. The G force can be over six times normal. To combat the effects, astronauts lie down during the early stages of take-off. This means that the G force acts from their chests to their backs.

If they were sitting upright during take-off there would be a risk that blood would not be able to reach their brains and they would faint.

Corkscrews

More and more exciting roller coasters have been built. Some roller coasters are called corkscrews. On these rides the passengers experience a force over three times normal gravity during the first drop.

One of the world's fastest roller coasters, the Magnum XL-2, in Ohio, USA, the cars reach a top speed of over 112 kilometres an hour. This is as fast as the speed limit on many motorways.

Falling force

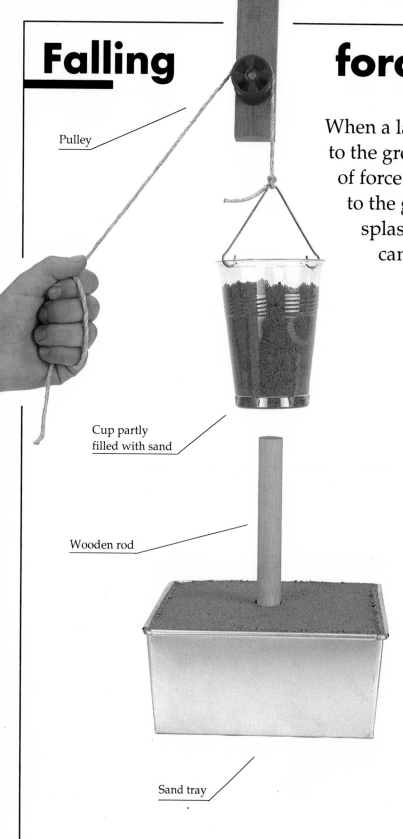

Pulley

Cup partly
filled with sand

Wooden rod

Sand tray

When a large weight falls freely
to the ground it lands with a lot
of force. Even a raindrop falling
to the ground produces a great
splash on impact. The results
can be quite startling.

Pile driver
A pile-driver is a machine
that uses a large falling
weight to knock concrete
foundations, or piles, into
the ground.

Piles are used to support
large buildings on soft soil.
But even a small weight can
create a large force when it
is allowed to drop. You can
try this with a cup of sand
on a string. Make up the
experiment shown in this
picture, by filling the cup
with sand and then running
the string over a pulley.

The wooden rod is placed
on a sand tray and the cup
hauled to its highest point.
When the string is released
the cup will fall and knock
the wood into the sand of
the sand tray.

Does each blow with this
falling hammer knock the
block the same amount
into the tray?

The falling axe

When people want to split timber they often use an axe. They raise the axe over their heads and then bring the axe head down on the timber with a great curving action. In this way the muscle power of the woodsman is made greater by the natural fall of the axe. The result is a wood smashing action that can soon turn even large trees into firewood.

Craters galore

If you drop a marble into some dry flour it will make a dent called a crater. Look carefully at the crater and you will see the sides stand up quite clearly. This is where the force of the marble has *pushed* the flour aside.

As the marble falls it also *splatters* flour over a wide distance. This is the effect of a fast impact, where some material was thrown out.

Both effects are the normal result of falling.

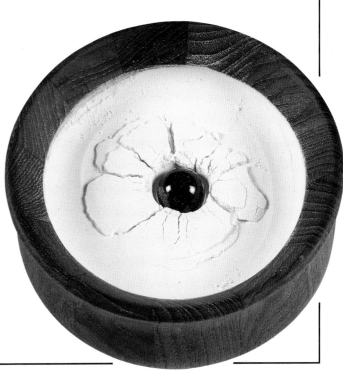

Bouncing

When something falls to the ground it usually bounces back – or rebounds – a little way. If you let a pencil drop onto a table you will see that it bounces before coming to rest.

We choose some materials simply because they bounce a lot. A rubber ball will bounce many times after it has fallen to the ground.

Bouncing balls
The bouncing power of a ball depends on the ball and also the surface onto which it falls.

Try this with a ball that you let fall from the same height each time. Let the ball fall on to concrete, wooden floorboards, a mat, grass and other surfaces.

Try to measure how high it bounces back up.

Jumping apple

This apple has a elastic band holding it to the beam. It has been dropped and is bouncing about. Can you see any pattern to the way it is bouncing? Can you think of any use this kind of bouncing could be put to?

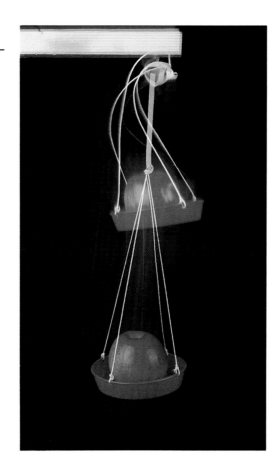

Changing shape

When this rider bounces down on the air-filled bag, it changes shape and squashes. This stores up the force of the fall. Then the bag rebounds, pushing the rider back up into the air. The result is a hopping motion. The rebounding principle is used in many types of springing devices such as trampolines. In a trampoline the force of falling is stored in the springs, which stretch and store the energy. They shorten again when the athlete's falling force is spent, throwing them back into the air.

Balancing weight

Heavy objects are difficult to move about. Balancing out the weight can be a useful way of measuring how much they weigh. It can also make heavy loads easier to move.

An apple weighs more than a pencil sharpener. If the apple and the sharpener are placed equal distances from the pivot this will happen

Find the balance

You can make a balance like the ones in these pictures. You need a ruler or stiff card with a scale on it and a pencil or triangle of wood to make the pivot.

Place the ruler so that its centre rests on the pivot. Put a small weight on one end. The weighted end will fall and the unweighted end will rise. If you press down on the unweighted end it will be easy to lift the weighted end off the table.

The lifting force of the ruler depends on where the weight is placed. If it is nearer the balancing point it will be easier to lift. This is how you can make a pencil sharpener lift an apple. But if a heavy weight is placed at the end of the ruler and you push down near the pivot the weight will be very difficult to lift.

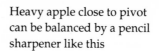

Heavy apple close to pivot can be balanced by a pencil sharpener like this

Carry the load

One way of carrying heavy loads is to divide them into two equal amounts and put them in baskets at the end of a pole. The weights are easier to carry when balanced than if they were all placed in a single bag.

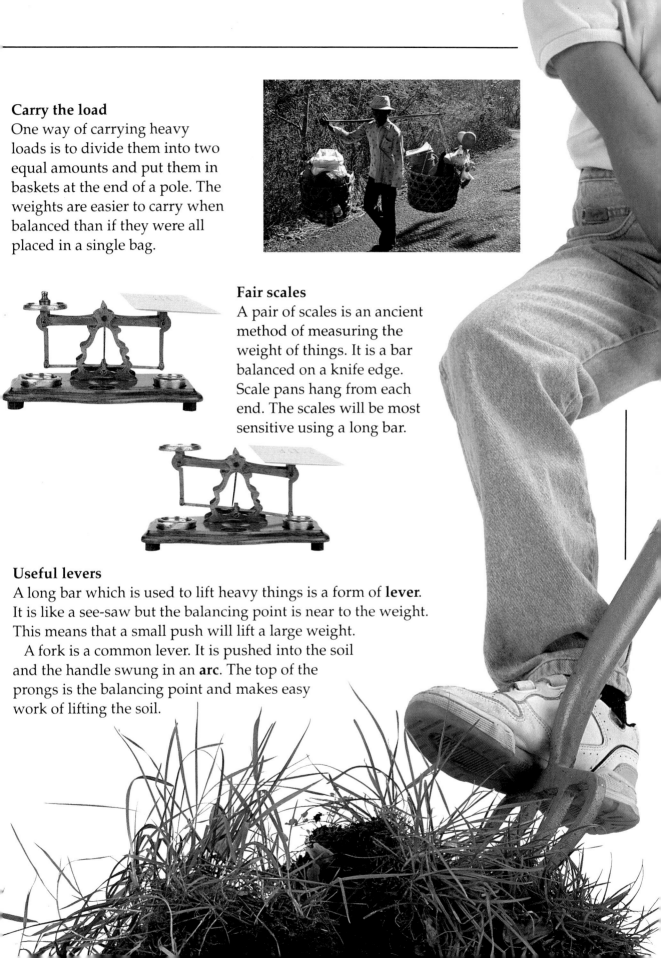

Fair scales

A pair of scales is an ancient method of measuring the weight of things. It is a bar balanced on a knife edge. Scale pans hang from each end. The scales will be most sensitive using a long bar.

Useful levers

A long bar which is used to lift heavy things is a form of **lever**. It is like a see-saw but the balancing point is near to the weight. This means that a small push will lift a large weight.

A fork is a common lever. It is pushed into the soil and the handle swung in an **arc**. The top of the prongs is the balancing point and makes easy work of lifting the soil.

Going up and down

Falling can be used to help reduce the effort needed to go upwards.

For example, the weight of a lift cage in a building can be balanced by a slab of concrete. This means that the lift motor only needs to pull the extra weight of any people using the lift and not the weight of the lift cage as well.

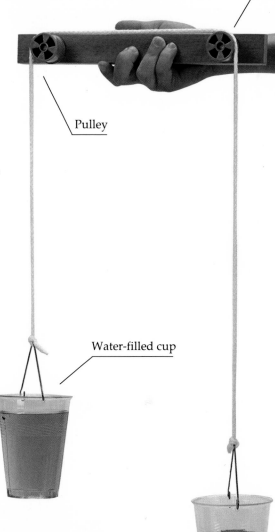

Pulley

Pulley

Water-filled cup

Sand-filled cup

Make a lift
See what happens when you tie two paper cups to a string and then place them over a pulley. An old cotton reel on a knitting needle makes a good pulley.

Half fill one cup with sand or another heavy material. The filled cup will stay firmly on the floor unless you pull down on the other.

Fill the empty cup with water until the sand cup just lifts off the ground. Now you can move both cups easily. You have used one weight to **counterbalance** another.

Nodding donkey

Much of the world's oil and water is brought from the ground using a pump called a nodding donkey. A nodding donkey rocks backwards and forwards using the pull of a machine at one end and the weight of the pump rod at the other.

Bridge opening

When a ship approaches Tower Bridge, which spans the River Thames in London, the two halves of the roadway are lifted.

Chambers in each tower are filled with water. As they fill the chambers balance the weight of the roadway and allow each half to tip up. When the ships have passed through, the water is pumped out of the chambers and the roadway falls again.

Swinging about

A pendulum is a falling weight that is held in place by a rod or chain. This means the pendulum cannot fall straight down, but has to fall in a curve called an arc.

Once it is set in motion a pendulum will swing backwards and forwards for a long time before it comes to rest.

Music-master

A metronome is used to help people keep time when playing music. The pendulum is kept inside a box. As it swings back and forth it catches against a plate and makes a ticking sound. The musician listens to the ticks to keep time while practising.

The speed of the pendulum is changed by sliding a small counterbalance weight up and down the pendulum arm.

Swing against the fall

A playground swing is a kind of pendulum. Find out how it works as you swing backwards and forwards.

In the falling part of the swing the pendulum gets faster. It arcs through the air and is fastest as it reaches the bottom of the swing.

As soon as the pendulum goes past the bottom of the stroke it is on the upward part of its curve. Here it slows down because it is working against gravity. It finally comes to a stop before starting to fall again.

Swinging speed

Pendulums have a very regular movement. In this picture the speed of the swing is changed by pushing the circular weight along the rod. But would you know which way to push the weight to make the clock run slower?

You can find out how the swing of a pendulum changes by using different lengths of string and a small weight.

Tie at half a metre long piece of string to a horizontal bar and fix a weight to the end. Tie a shorter pendulum near to the first and start them swinging together. Watch what happens. Which swings more slowly – a long pendulum or a short one?

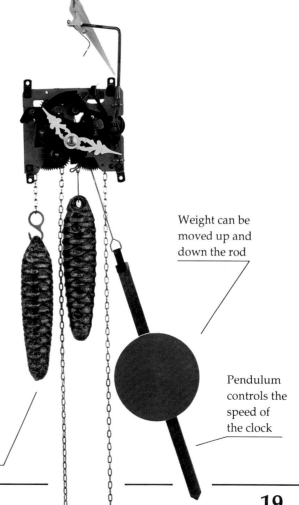

Weight can be moved up and down the rod

Pendulum controls the speed of the clock

Falling weights drive the clock

19

Stretching

Some materials will stretch if they are pulled. Rubber and some ropes are examples of materials that will bend or stretch when pulled and squashed when pressed, but spring back when released. They are called **elastic** materials.

Elastic materials are easily stretched by gravity when objects are fixed to them. Many elastic materials stretch in a very regular way.

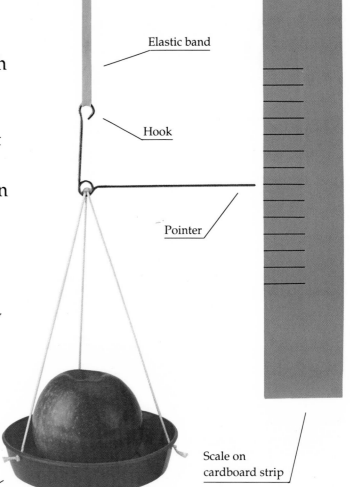

Hook

Elastic band

Hook

Pointer

Scale on cardboard strip

Pan to hold objects that are to be weighed

Stretch balance
To make a stretch balance bend a piece of wire into a hook and pointer. Slip an elastic band through the hook just like the picture above. Then make a scale pan from a jar top and some thread.

When an object is put on the scale-pan the weight tries to fall to the ground and this stretches the elastic band. If you put things of known weight on scale pan you will be able to work out a scale for the pointer. Try using packets that have the weight printed on the side.

Controlling the stretch

Ropes can be designed to give just the right amount of stretch. These people are **abseiling** – jumping down the cliff using special equipment. The rope is designed to help them jump down in a smooth even way.

Portable scales

It is very important to make sure that small babies get enough food and put on weight properly. In country areas, away from hospitals and doctor's surgeries this may not be easy.

In this example you can see the sling that is used to hold the baby while its weight is measured. However, the picture has been cut off so that you cannot see the scales that have been used.

Could you design a scale that would measure a baby's weight? The scales have to be easy to carry around and they must use a sling like the one shown.

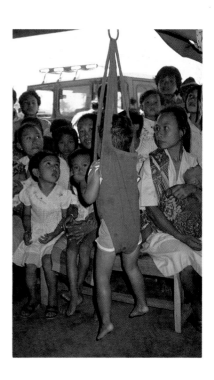

All slide down

Falling – being pulled down by gravity – doesn't always mean you have to go straight down. Every time an object slides or rolls down a slope it is 'falling'. Here the sudden drop of a fall – and the possible crash at the bottom – is replaced by a slower fall that is easier to control.

Water slide
A water slide is great fun. The large slide shown here is in Japan.

The corkscrew slide also makes sure that we arrive at the bottom quite safely. This is because the corkscrew makes the journey longer and the slope gentler.

To see the effect, take a piece of string and wind it corkscrew-fashion around a bottle.

Hairpin bends

Some roads in mountainous places are very steep. If a road was built straight down a mountain slope without having any bends in it, a car would go so fast that the brakes would not work well enough to slow it down. It would, in fact, rush out of control.

To make the slope less steep, the road is built with bends. Often these look like hairpins and are called 'hairpin bends'.

Roller castle

You can make a sand castle that easily shows the way that a winding ramp spreads out the effects of falling, making descent easier.

Make a tall cone-shaped castle and then make a spiral groove round the outside, slightly bigger than a marble. The finished castle is shown in this picture.

Marbles placed at the top of the castle roll smoothy down to the bottom. It is the same way a water slide works.

Toppling

Tall objects often topple over as they fall.

When a tree is felled for timber or when a storm blows a tree down, the top of the tree will swing in a great arc, while the bottom of the tree will move just a little.

As the tree arcs through the air it is likely that it will hit other trees or houses in its path. This can easily cause a lot of damage.

Toppling dominoes
You can experiment with domino toppling. Stand some dominoes on edge and close to each other. Push one gently so it topples and begins to knock the others over.

You might like to see what patterns you can make with dominoes.

Pencil test
A pencil on its end will fall rather like a tree. To find out what happens put some flour in a tray and carefully smooth it out. Then stand a pencil upright in the centre of the tray and let it fall.

Look at the mark made where the pencil fell. Where does the deepest dent (and therefore the greatest force) seem to be?

World score

Some types of toppling can be controlled. People have made domino toppling a great sport.

The most dominoes to be toppled by a single gentle push was nearly 300 000. They took twelve minutes to fall down.

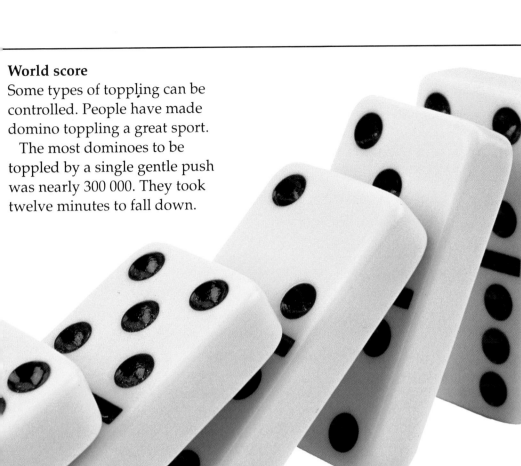

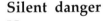

Silent danger

Houses can easily be damaged by nearby falling trees. Old trees are the most dangerous because their roots are starting to decay and weaken.

All fall down

The 'domino' effect of trees can cause severe damage in a forest. Look at these trees that were felled by a storm. The storm only directly toppled the ones in the front. All the others were knocked over as the first trees fell into them.

Falling water

Water spilling over a waterfall and crashing on the rocks below has great power. Some of the world's largest waterfalls, such as the Niagara Falls on the border between the USA and Canada, have power to provide the electricity needs of a big city. The problem for science is how to harness it.

Make a water-wheel

You can easily make your own water-wheel and see how falling water has the power to drive it. You just need a cardboard tube or cotton reel and a sheet of flat card.

The cardboard tube or cotton reel will be the centre of the wheel. Get a grown-up to help you score slits in the tube. These will take the paddles of the water-wheel. Push strips of stiff card into the slits like these in the picture. You can use as many strips as you like.

Use a piece of wooden rod (a dowel stick) to go through the tube and make a spindle. Alternatively you can use wire (from an old clothes hanger) like the model shown here.

When you put the wheel under a running tap you will find the wheel spins very fast and is quite hard to stop.

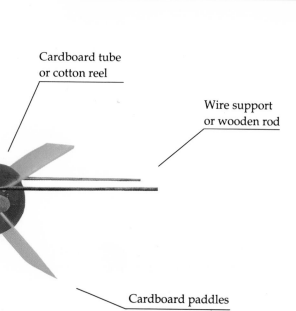

Cardboard tube or cotton reel

Wire support or wooden rod

Cardboard paddles

Water -mill
People have used the power of running water to work machines for thousands of years. The power is captured from a river using a wheel. Usually the wheel is fitted with many wide blades which catch the water and spin readily.

Power stations
The world's big power stations no longer use open water wheels. Instead, they trap the water in a pipe.

There is a special kind of wheel in the pipe that looks rather like the water wheel you have made. It has many sets of blades and is called a turbine.

Using falling water to make electricity in this way is called hydro-electric power. Falling water produces clean and unpolluting electric energy.

Falling gently

Although you cannot see air, it is a **gas** and just like water it has resistance. When something moves it must push the air out of the way. The resistance of the air to being moved is called the drag.

A parachute has a very large surface area to give it a big drag and make it fall slowly and steadily.

Wobbling
Shuttlecocks fall slowly through the air because the 'feathers' round their edges make them catch the air.

Try dropping a shuttlecock and you will see that it wobbles as it falls. Wobbling is common to many falling objects: when a feather or a leaf wobbles as it falls we call it fluttering.

Parachutes would be very difficult to control if they wobbled. To stop wobbling there is a hole in the middle of the parachute. This allows some air to flow smoothly through the parachute rather than seeking a way out each side.

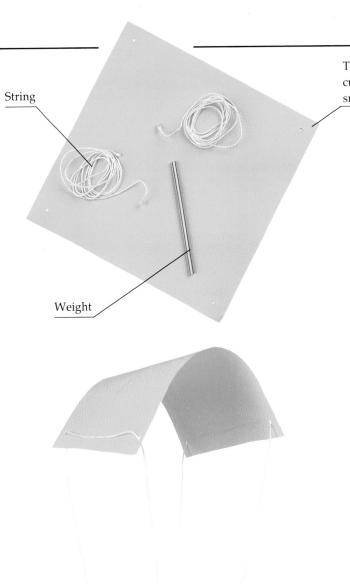

String

Thin paper or cloth cut to a square. Four small holes in corners

Weight

Make a parachute

A parachute is a way of slowing down a fall. You can make a parachute from a large copy of this pattern. Use thin paper such as kitchen towel or lightweight fabric such as cotton.

Tie a piece of thread to each corner and bring all the threads together at the centre. Knot the threads around a weight, such as a piece of Plasticine or a stone. Then let the parachute fall.

Many real parachutes are rectangular rather than circular and have 'L'-shaped slots cut off centre. This lets the air flow in a special way and can make for a more controlled landing. You can try experimenting with different shapes of parachute.

Falling naturally

Nature has found many ways of using falling to advantage. Some plants have seeds that are especially designed for falling through the air. Some animals have such quick reactions that they can turn as they fall.

Caution:
Never drop any animal to see how it falls. This picture was taken by experts who made sure the animal could come to no harm

Quick turn
Animals that live high in trees could injure themselves if they fell to the ground in an uncontrolled way.

Some animals have long tails which they wrap round branches to act as a safety line. Others make sure they fall on their feet and use their legs as shock absorbers.

A cat has very fast reactions. This means that even if it should fall, it has a good chance of landing safely. As a cat falls it first turns the front of its body, and then the rear. Then it stretches out its legs. Finally it starts to dive slightly so that its front legs reach the ground before the rear ones. All these movements help to ensure a soft and safe landing.

Spinning to new land

Maple and sycamore seeds are among those that have a special shape. The heavy seed sits between the wings. When the seed falls from the tree the air rushes past the wings and they start to turn.

The spinning wings make the seed fall more slowly and it is easily caught by the wind and blown clear of the tree.

Stick in the mud

Trees can make good use of falling to help spread their seeds. Some seeds are shaped specially to help them as they fall. These mangrove seeds are heavier at the thicker end. This means they always fall the right way up.

The seeds are also shaped like spears. By the time they reach the ground they are falling fast and the spear shape helps to punch a hole in the soft mud.

Shaking down

Secrets of sand castles

Would you make a sand castle out of dry sand or wet sand?

Make a sand castle with as steep side as you can out of dry sand. See if you can find a way of measuring how steep it is.

Next, make a sand castle in wet sand. Notice how the water is acting as a kind of cement, sticking all the sand grains together. Try shaking gently the pile of dry sand and then the sand castle made of wet sand. Which collapses first?

Investigate piles of sugar, flour, soil and other loose materials. Do they all behave in the same way?

When is a slope in danger of falling down and hurting people? Many disasters have been caused by falling rocks or soil. Here are some clues on what makes a slope start to fall – and how to stop it.

Side falls away because it is less well held by water

Much of the sand castle stays intact

Part of the fallen block stays intact

Some of the fallen sand is scattered about

Disaster!

Snow can be a loose material. When it is piled high by snowstorms it can build up into very steep slopes. This is the cause of **avalanches** like the one shown in this picture.

Steep piles of snow can be shaken by something as small as a shout or a gunshot. Once disturbed thousands of tonnes of snow can fall down a mountainside, rushing to the bottom faster than the speed of an express train and destroying any buildings in its path.

Nature's sand castles

This are sand dunes in a desert. The surface is covered with small ridges called ripples. Sand dunes are really just huge piles of sand that have been piled up by the wind. Look to see if the steepest slopes have a similar angle to the dry sand you have piled up.

Staying upright

If we want things to stand up we have to know about the way they can fall over. This means we need to know how the weight is spread out in the object.

If the weight is mostly near the ground an object will be much more stable than if the weight is near the top.

Rolling back

If you look at the toys made for your younger brothers or sisters or for your pets you will see many of them have been made to stay upright.

If you pick up this kind of toy it feels very heavy with most of the weight near the bottom. This is called a low **centre of gravity**. The round bottom is also important. It means that the toy can be knocked to one side and still roll upright again.

Ancient error

This famous building is the Leaning Tower of Pisa in Italy. When it was completed it stood upright, but the ground underneath was weak and the building has slowly settled into the ground on one side. It has not fallen over yet because it is still not 'top heavy'.

Fall-proof shape

Some shapes are more likely to stay upright, or be stable, than others. These are the ones where most of the weight is low down. The pyramids at Giza in Egypt (shown in this picture) are a good example of a very stable shape.

See if you can find the shape that is hardest to knock over. Make a number of shapes using building blocks.

Try to knock each one over using a ball on a string. Use the ball like a pendulum so it always hits the shape with the same force.

Building for safety

Modern cars go very fast but they are more stable than old cars that went much more slowly.

Look at the cars of the past and you can see how they were much higher. A modern car has the weight down between the wheels. This means that the car is less liable to roll over on a bend.

The most stable cars are racing cars. Here the driver is almost lying flat between the wheels.

The longest throw

When we throw something, such as a snowball, gravity will make it fall to the ground. To break the world records, the best athletes have found ways to work against gravity for as long as possible.

Like the best athletes, you can try to improve your performance by thinking carefully about the way an object curves through the air when it has been thrown.

Curving path

All athletic field events use the idea of **projectiles**. This means that athletes try to throw the shot, discus, javelin or themselves in a long sweeping curve.

You can see the idea when you try to throw a ball a long way. You reason that it is sensible to throw the ball level to go as far as possible. But gravity will soon bring the ball to the ground. So you have to angle the throw upwards just enough to make the ball go as far as possible before it hits the ground. Getting the right angle needs practise and skill.

All projectiles make
a curving path through
the air like this one

The javelin throw

The javelin is a special pole with a pointed end. It is an athlete's spear. It is held in the hand and released in a long curving path.

The trick is to make the javelin go on a gently curving path.

Look carefully to see the angle that this athlete is throwing his javelin. It is much steeper than the angle you would throw a ball, but it is correct for this long projectile.

The record throw of a javelin is nearly 105 metres.

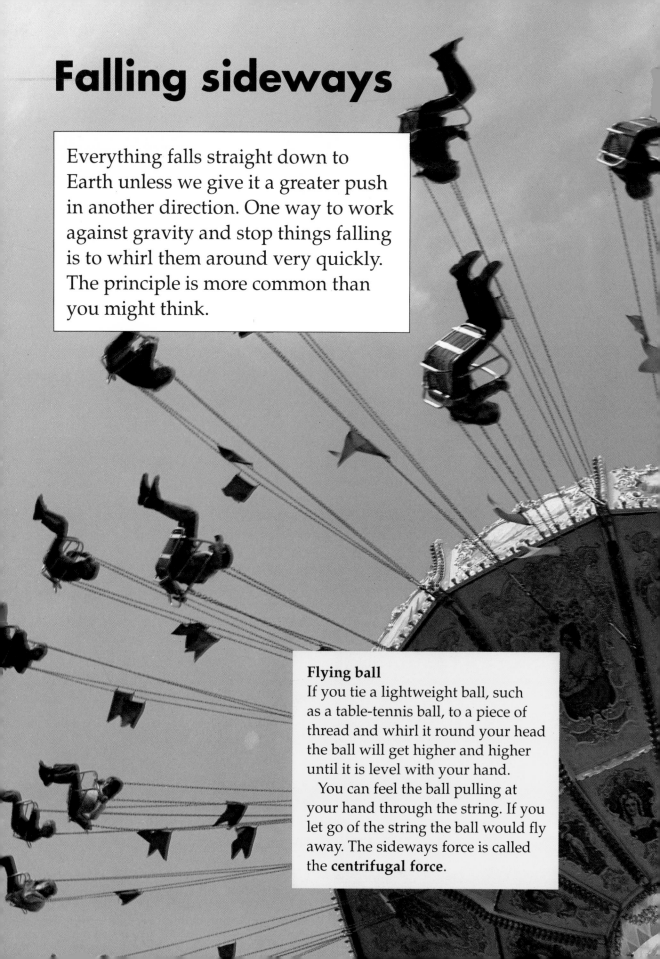

Falling sideways

Everything falls straight down to Earth unless we give it a greater push in another direction. One way to work against gravity and stop things falling is to whirl them around very quickly. The principle is more common than you might think.

Flying ball
If you tie a lightweight ball, such as a table-tennis ball, to a piece of thread and whirl it round your head the ball will get higher and higher until it is level with your hand.

You can feel the ball pulling at your hand through the string. If you let go of the string the ball would fly away. The sideways force is called the **centrifugal force**.

Spinning wheels

Some fairground machines work in the same way as the whirling ball or the spin-drier you use to dry clothes. People sit in special cars and the machine begins to spin. If you go for a ride in these cars you will feel yourself pushed more and more firmly into your seat.

Satellites

A satellite is a kind of whirling ball. As it goes round, or **orbits**, the Earth it tries to fly out into space. At the same time gravity is pulling it to the ground. The effect is just the same as if there were a string tying the satellite to the Earth.

Scientists choose how high the satellite will orbit by choosing the speed it travels.

The Solar System

Look out into space on a clear night and you will see thousands of twinkling lights. Most of them are **stars** a very long way away.

Around our star, the Sun, there is a cluster of nine planets. The Sun and its planets make up the Solar System. The Solar System is held together by the force of gravity which balances the spinning, or centrifugal force of each planet.

Caution:
Never try to look at the Sun with binoculars or a telescope. It could seriously damage your eyes and even cause blindness.

Asteroids
(fragments of rock)

Mars
(red)

Earth
(blue)

Venus
(white)

Sun
(yellow)

Mercury

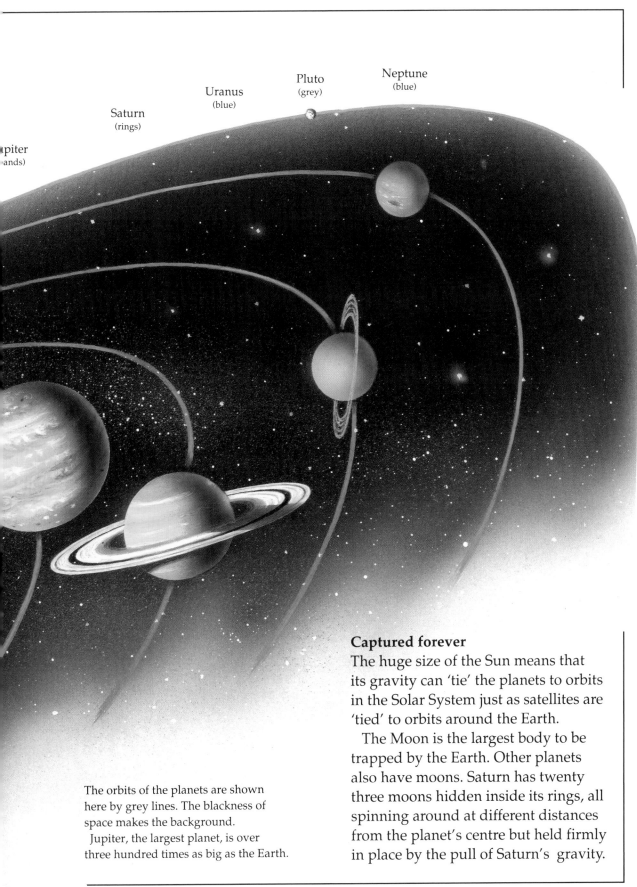

Jupiter
(bands)

Saturn
(rings)

Uranus
(blue)

Pluto
(grey)

Neptune
(blue)

Captured forever

The huge size of the Sun means that its gravity can 'tie' the planets to orbits in the Solar System just as satellites are 'tied' to orbits around the Earth.

The Moon is the largest body to be trapped by the Earth. Other planets also have moons. Saturn has twenty three moons hidden inside its rings, all spinning around at different distances from the planet's centre but held firmly in place by the pull of Saturn's gravity.

The orbits of the planets are shown here by grey lines. The blackness of space makes the background.

Jupiter, the largest planet, is over three hundred times as big as the Earth.

Meteorites

A **meteorite**, also known as a falling or shooting star, is the streak of light you occasionally see in the night-time sky. It is produced when a large piece of rock from space gets captured by the Earth's gravity and falls towards the ground. The light happens because the rock burns up as it rushes through the Earth's atmosphere.

Meteor crater
Meteor Crater in the USA shows how big an effect they can have. This meteorite was just 30 metres across, but it fell so fast (over 16 kilometres a second) that it made a crater more than 1 kilometre across.

It hit the ground with such force it even turned some of the rocks into tiny diamonds.

Why meteorites fall

As the Sun and the planets sweep through space their gravity captures many meteorites. The Earth is still growing as it sweeps through space capturing meteorites.

The largest meteorites do not burn up entirely, but crash on the Earth's surface where they make huge craters.

Meteorites and craters

Meteorites have had a very important effect on the Moon because it is not protected by an atmosphere. As a result all the meteorites that fall to its surface make big craters. The largest craters are over 1000 kilometres across and you can clearly see them from Earth.

Look at the Moon through a telescope or binoculars. Although the largest craters were possibly made by volcanoes, most craters were probably made by meteorites.

Living without gravity

It is difficult to imagine a world with no gravity. There would be nothing to hold your feet to the ground. As soon as you walked you would drift helplessly into the air and out into space.

The Earth has a strong gravity, but in other places, such as the Moon, gravity is much weaker. In space there is very little gravity at all.

The effects of weightlessness
It is not easy to get used to weightless flight. Many people find they feel 'travel sick' because of the unusual ease of moving about.

We use fluid in our ears to help us get a sense of balance and also to decide which way is up. Without gravity new ways of feeling 'upright' have to be found.

Walking on the Moon
The Moon has a gravitational pull about a tenth as strong as the Earth. This makes it much easier to move about. However, when astronauts visited the Moon they found that a movement that would have been a small hop on Earth became a giant leap and they had to find a new way of walking.

Spacewalking

A weightless world can be a dangerous world. When an astronaut goes out from the spacecraft there is great danger of just drifting out into space. To stop this astronauts have to wear a special rocket engine pack or use a lifeline.

Living in space

The rules of moving that can be used on Earth cannot be used in space. Tools have to be held in special ways or tied by lines or Velcro pads. Otherwise there is a danger that a floating spanner will simply float away.

Eating and drinking are also very difficult in space. There is not enough gravity to help liquids 'fall' into your mouth or to pour a drink into a cup. Liquids have to be squeezed into the mouths of the astronauts through a tube, and they have to push solids into their mouths – a fork or spoon is useless.

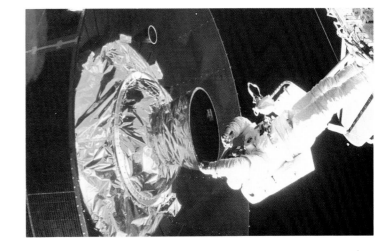

New words

abseil

is used by people when they want to get down a cliff very quickly. They make a series of jumps down the cliff, using the rope to support their weight. It is very important to use a rope with just the right amount of stretch or the rope might break

arc

a small part of a circle

avalanche

the rapid movement of a huge mass of snow down a mountainside. Avalanches can reach speeds for hundreds of kilometres and hour and they can cause great damage to any buildings that lie in their paths

centre of gravity

it is often useful to try to work out the place where the real weight of an object lies. The term centre of gravity is used to describe this place. If the object has most of its weight high up, it is probably 'top heavy'. It has its centre of gravity high up. If the weight is mostly low down, it is 'bottom heavy' with a centre of gravity low down. This position makes an object much less likely to fall over

centrifugal force

when an object whirls round and round it always tries to fly outwards and away from its orbit. Many people call the effect the centrifugal force

counterbalance

when an object is balanced there must be the same weight on both sides of the pivoting point. A counterbalance is a weight that is added to a machine to get it into balance. Counterbalances are found in many places. They could be found as a weight on the end of a bar, or a weight on the end of a pulley

force

in Nature most objects do not move without help. To make them move some effort has to be applied. Perhaps the effort is pulling or pushing. There are many kinds of effort. Each one is a force

gas

an substance that is a vapour. Many gases, such as oxygen, are invisible. The main gases of the air are nitrogen, hydrogen and oxygen

gravity

this is the force produced by every object in the Universe. The force of gravity depends on the size of the object. If the object is the size of a marble, the gravity force is has is too tiny to notice. But when the object is the size of a planet, its gravity force is huge

lever
this is a long bar which is used to help people to make light work of moving a heavy object. The lever is used with a pivot. The lever is placed under the heavy weight and over the pivot. The weight is lifted by pressing down on the other end of the lever

mass
this is the amount of matter in an object. Scientists use the word mass to talk about the amount of matter in an object because its weight changes with the force of gravity. A ball has the same mass on the Earth and on the Moon, but its weight will be much greater on the Earth where gravity is stronger. The mass of an object is measured in units called kilogrammes

meteorite
these are pieces of rock that are scattered in space. It was pieces of rock like meteorites that originally made up the planets in the Solar system. The Earth draws meteorites towards it all the time. Most of them weight just a few kilogrammes and they burn up in the atmosphere to give shooting stars. It is rare for a meteorite to land on Earth

orbit
this is the path made by a body that whirls round a fixed point. A ball on the end of a string makes a circular orbit as it whirls round. Most satellites make a nearly circular orbit as they go round the Earth, although some orbit in an oval shape

projectile
this is any object that is thrown or shot into the air. The projectile might be an arrow, a stone, a ball or a bullet. All make the same type of curving path as they fly through the air

space
the region beyond the Earth's atmosphere containing all the planets and stars. It is often used to mean the Universe except for the Earth

star
stars are balls of intensely hot liquid and gas. Our Sun is a small star compared with many in the Universe. Stars are so hot that no solid rock can form

Universe
the Universe is the name for everything that we know to exist, the Earth, the Sun, and all the other stars, planets and space beyond them

weight
objects have a weight due to gravity. A table tennis ball and a lump of lead of the same size will weight different amounts because of gravity. The weight of an object is measured in units called Newtons

Index